MELISSA ETHERIDGE

GREATEST HITS

Cover photo by Dan Winters

ISBN 978-0-634-04581-3

HAL•LEONARD®
CORPORATION

7777 W. BLUEMOUND RD. P.O. BOX 13819 MILWAUKEE, WI 53213

STRUM IT GUITAR LEGEND

Strum It is the series designed especially to get you playing (and singing!) along with your favorite songs. The idea is simple – the songs are arranged using their original keys in lead sheet format, providing you with the authentic chords for each song, beginning to end. Rhythm slashes are written above the staff. Strum the chords in the rhythm indicated. Use the chord diagrams found at the top of the first page of the arrangement for the appropriate chord voicings. The melody and lyrics are also shown to help you keep your spot and sing along.

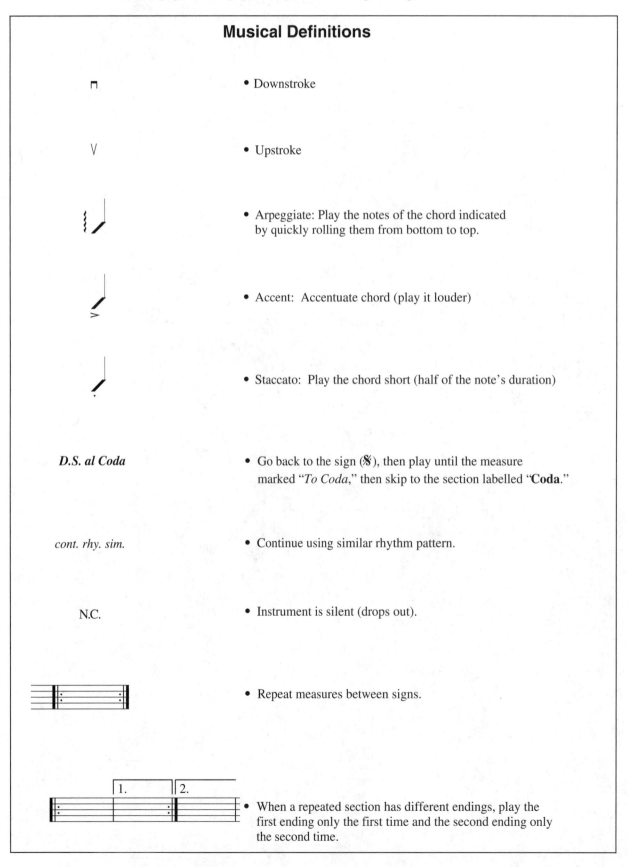

Musical Definitions

- Downstroke

- Upstroke

- Arpeggiate: Play the notes of the chord indicated by quickly rolling them from bottom to top.

- Accent: Accentuate chord (play it louder)

- Staccato: Play the chord short (half of the note's duration)

D.S. al Coda
- Go back to the sign (𝄋), then play until the measure marked "*To Coda*," then skip to the section labelled "**Coda**."

cont. rhy. sim.
- Continue using similar rhythm pattern.

N.C.
- Instrument is silent (drops out).

- Repeat measures between signs.

1.   2.
- When a repeated section has different endings, play the first ending only the first time and the second ending only the second time.

Ain't It Heavy

Words and Music by Melissa Etheridge

1. Some - times _ I know that it's
   2. See additional lyrics

nev - er e - nough. _ Sur - vi - val is fine, _ but sat - is - fac - tion is rough. I _

___ try with an an - gel to - night. _ Spread _

To Coda
Badd4
Aadd9
E
Esus4
Heav - y, ain't it heav - y. Ain't the night heav - y.
Interlude
E
D sus2 add6
C#m7
Asus2
1.
2.
D.S. al Coda
E
2. I'm feel -
Coda
Interlude
E
D sus2 add6
C#m7
Asus2
F#m7add4
Asus2
E

Additional Lyrics

2. I'm feelin' kinda loose, I'm feelin' kinda mean.
   I've been feelin' kinda wild since I turned seventeen.
   Or is it madness?
   Tell me, where can a woman find any kind of peace.
   When does the fury and the agony cease?
   How long have I got to say please?
   There's a hole in my jeans; I only wanted to fade.
   I've been ripping out seams somebody else made tonight.

All American Girl

Words and Music by Melissa Etheridge

1. She wakes up in the morn - ing with a pain in her jet ___ black head. ___

2. *See additional lyrics*

De - caf cof - fee in her hand ___ and a Marl - bor - o red. ___

She drives — down to the of - fice in her

Jap - a - nese — car — with the ra - di - o — blast - ing. She dreams of

tak - in' it — too far (But) to - day she'll pay — the bills She won't

think a - bout — the thrills — that pass — a - way. — She's an

Chorus

all _____ A - mer - i - can — girl, _____

an — all _____ A - mer - i - can — girl.

She will live and die — in this man's —

To Coda ⊕

B5   N.C.   E   A   D

_____ world, _____ an all A - mer - i - can _____ girl. _____

D.S. al Coda

A   E   A   D   A

_____   2. Her eyes _____

⊕ Coda

Half-time feel

C   G

_____ girl. _____

D

Interlude

End half-time feel

A   Asus4   A   E   A   D

Spoken: All   right.

A   E   A   D   A

cont. rhy. sim.

Oh, yeah.   Come on.   Oh.

Verse

lov - er nev - er came home and it's half past three. To -

day her best friend told her he's H. I. V. Some-thing's

got - ta give some - where. Forc - ing cir - cles in - to squares,

she keeps push - ing on. She's an

Chorus

all A - mer - i - can girl,

cont. rhy. sim.

Oo, yeah. 3. Her

Additional Lyrics

2. Her eyes are black as leather,
   And her hair is killer red.
   How could she keep the baby
   When she can barely keep her head?
   She don't owe nobody nothin'
   And she ain't on the street.
   But these drinks are gettin' heavy
   And these tips are getting weak.
   And she don't understand why she can't
   Climb out of the sand and break away.

Come to My Window

Words and Music by Melissa Etheridge

Cadd9   G/B   D   Dsus2   D Dsus2

Cadd9   G/B   D   Dsus2

Verse

Cadd9   G/B   D   Dsus2

1. I would dial the num - bers just to lis - ten to your breath. And

Cadd9   G/B   D   Dsus2   D Dsus2

I would stand in - side my hell and hold the hand of death.

Cadd9   G/B   D   Dsus4 D Dsus2

You don't know how far I'd go to ease this pre-cious ache. And

Cadd9   G/B   D

you don't know how much I'd give or how much I can take. Just to reach

Em   Cadd9   D   Dsus4   D

you. Just to reach you. Oh, to

Angels Would Fall

Words and Music by Melissa Etheridge and John Shanks

18

Gm (Em)   E♭ (C)   B♭ (G)   F/A (D/F#)

des - per - ate hour, ___ it's bet - ter, bet - ter that way. ___

𝄋 Pre-Chorus

Cm (Am)   B♭/D (G/B)   E♭ (C)   F (D)   Gm (Em)

___ 1. So I'll ___ come by and see you a - gain. ___
2., 3. *See additional lyrics*

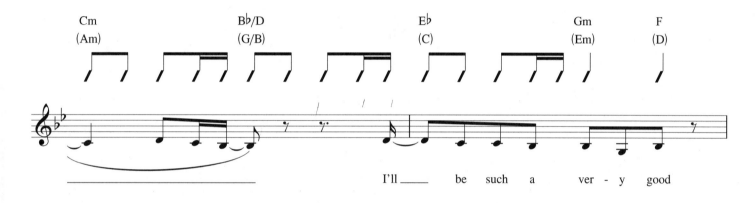

Cm (Am)   B♭/D (G/B)   E♭ (C)   Gm (Em)   F (D)

_____ I'll ___ be such a ver - y good

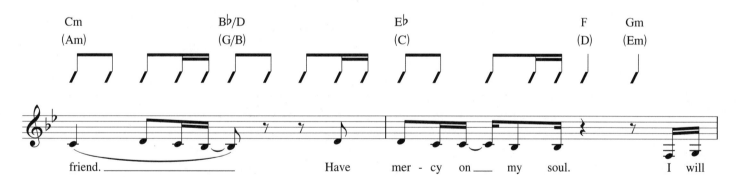

Cm (Am)   B♭/D (G/B)   E♭ (C)   F (D)   Gm (Em)

friend. _____ Have mer - cy on ___ my soul. I will

To Coda 1 ⊕

B♭maj7/F (Gmaj7/D)   E♭ (C)

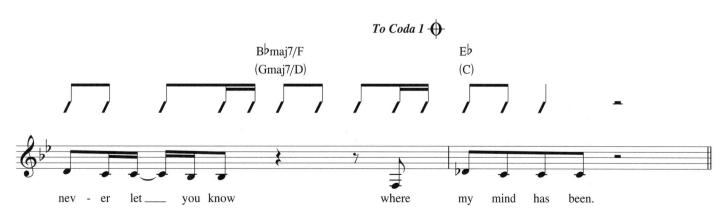

nev - er let ___ you know where my mind has been.

⊕ **Coda 2**

Outro
w/ Voc. ad lib., till fade

Repeat and fade

Additional Lyrics

2. I've crept into your temple. I have slept upon your pew.
   I have dreamed of the divinity inside and out of you.
   I want it more than truth. I can taste it on my breath.
   I would give my life just for a little, a little death.

Pre-Chorus 2. So, I'll come by and see you again.
   I'll be just a very good friend.
   I will not look upon your face.
   I will not touch upon your grace,
   Your ecclesiastic skin.

Pre-Chorus 3. I'll come by and see you again.
   And I'll have to be a very good friend.
   If I whisper they will know.
   I'll just turn around and go.
   You will never know my sin.

Bring Me Some Water

Words and Music by Melissa Etheridge

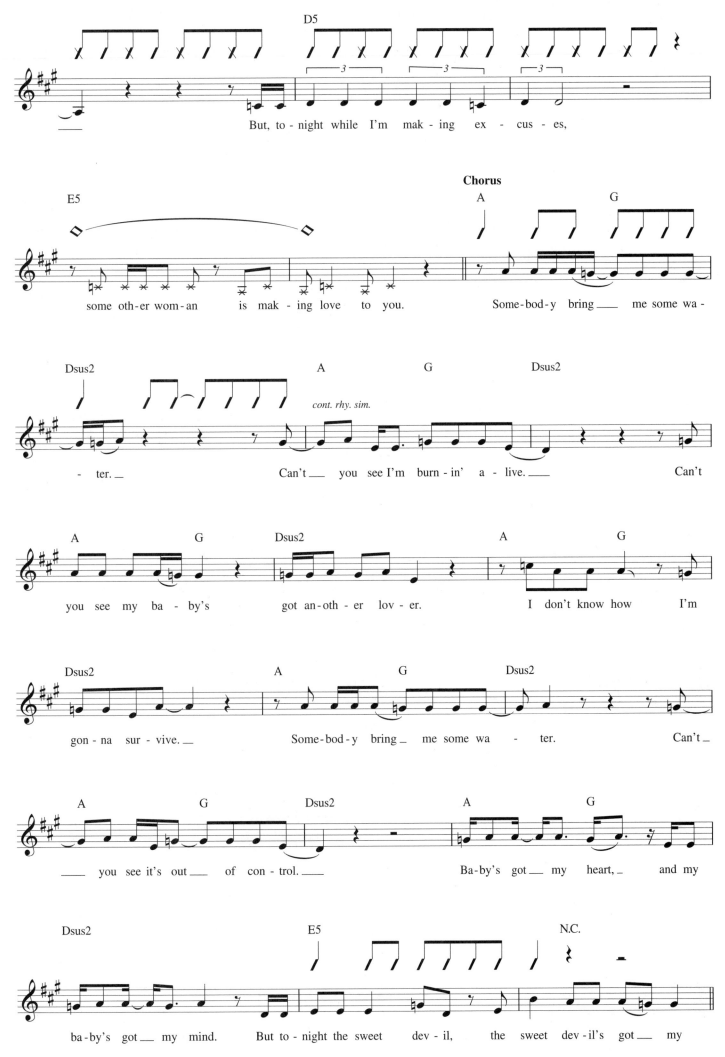

Dance Without Sleeping

Words and Music by Melissa Etheridge, Mauricio Fritz Lewak and Kevin McCormick

*Symbols in parentheses represent chord names respective to capoed guitar.
Symbols above reflect actual sounding chords.

1. I don't want to talk — a - bout — it.   I've done e-nough, I —

— think.   Don't want to   spend — more   mon - ey. —

Dance till I think I ___ can o - ver - come. ___

To Coda ⊕

Verse

2. Walk - ing on the edge ___ of rage and un - der - stand - ing,

cont. rhy. sim.

be - tween ___ the black ___ and ___ the white. ___

This child is ___ so an - gry, ___ a - lone here

to - night. A - larm - ing ___ des - per - a - tion

leads me to be - lieve, _____ with all ___ my ___ shields ___ and ___

D.S. al Coda

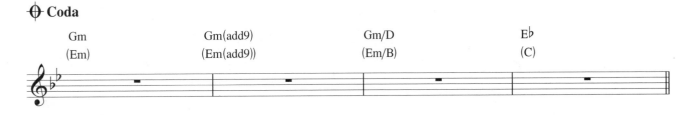

_____ pro - tec - tion, it's on - ly me ___ I de - ceive. ___

⊕ Coda

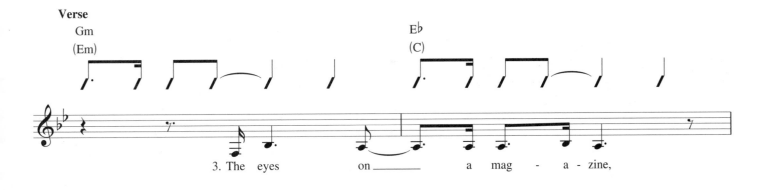

Verse

3. The eyes on _____ a mag - a - zine,

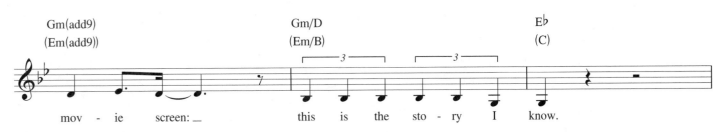

the voice on _____ the ra - di - o, the kiss _____ on the

mov - ie screen: _____ this is the sto - ry I know.

I Want to Come Over

Words and Music by Melissa Etheridge

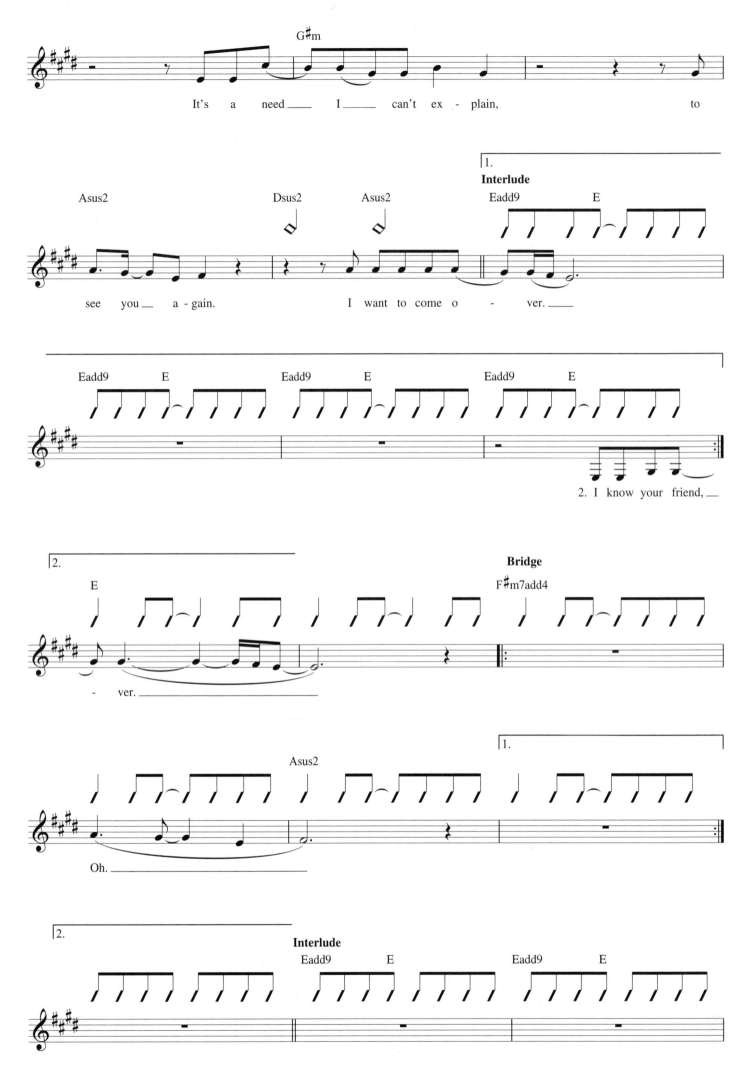

If I Wanted To

Words and Music by Melissa Etheridge

Oh, ___ oh. ___

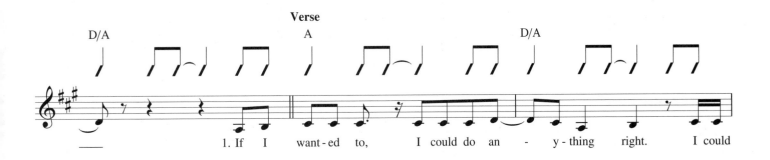

___ Oh, ___ oh. ___ Oh, ___ oh. ___ Oh, ___ oh. ___

Verse

___ 1. If I want-ed to, I could do an - y-thing right. I could

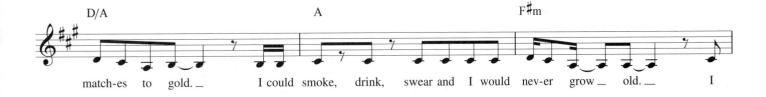

dance with the dev-il on a Sat-ur-day ___ night. ___ If I want-ed to, I could turn

match-es to gold. ___ I could smoke, drink, swear and I would nev-er grow ___ old. ___ I

would-n't have __ to be __ in __ love __ with you. __

If I on - ly want - ed to. __   Hey, if I on - ly want-

Verse

- ed to. __   2. If I want-ed to,   I could run fast __

___ as a train, __ be as sharp as a nee-dle that's twist-ing your brain. __ If I

want-ed to,   I could turn moun-tains to sand, __ have po - lit-i-cal lead-ers   in the

palm of my hand. __   I would-n't have __ to be ___ in love __ with you. __

___   If I on - ly want-ed to. __

Verse

I'm the Only One

Words and Music by Melissa Etheridge

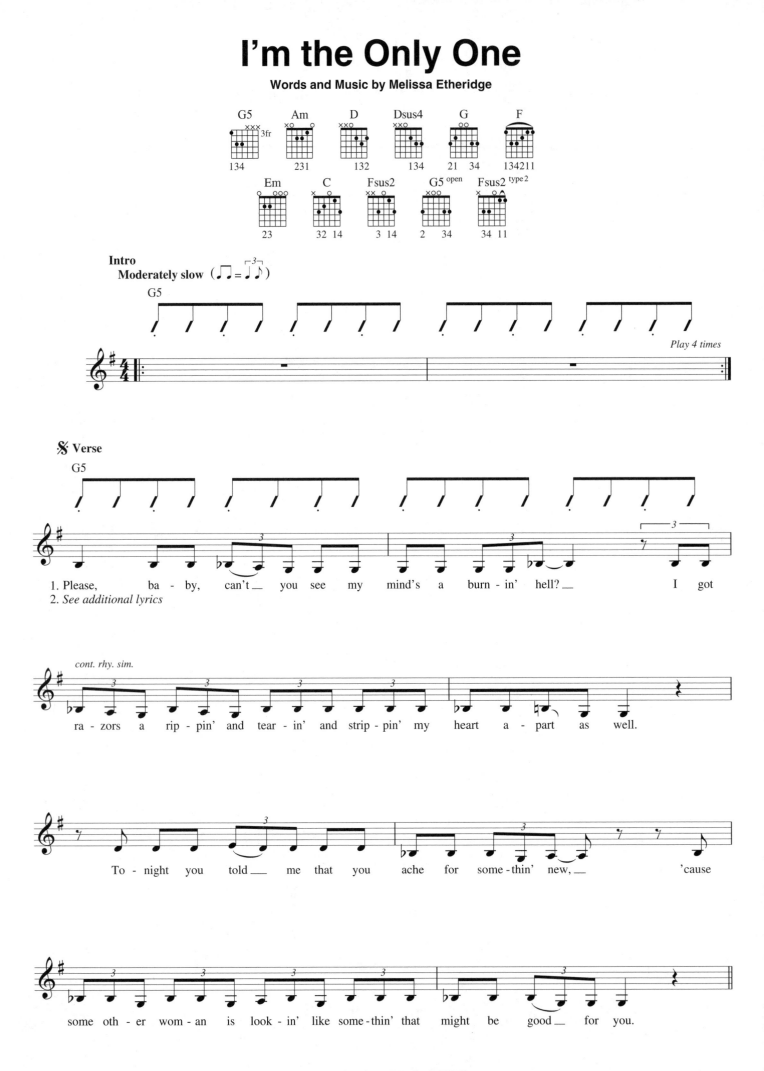

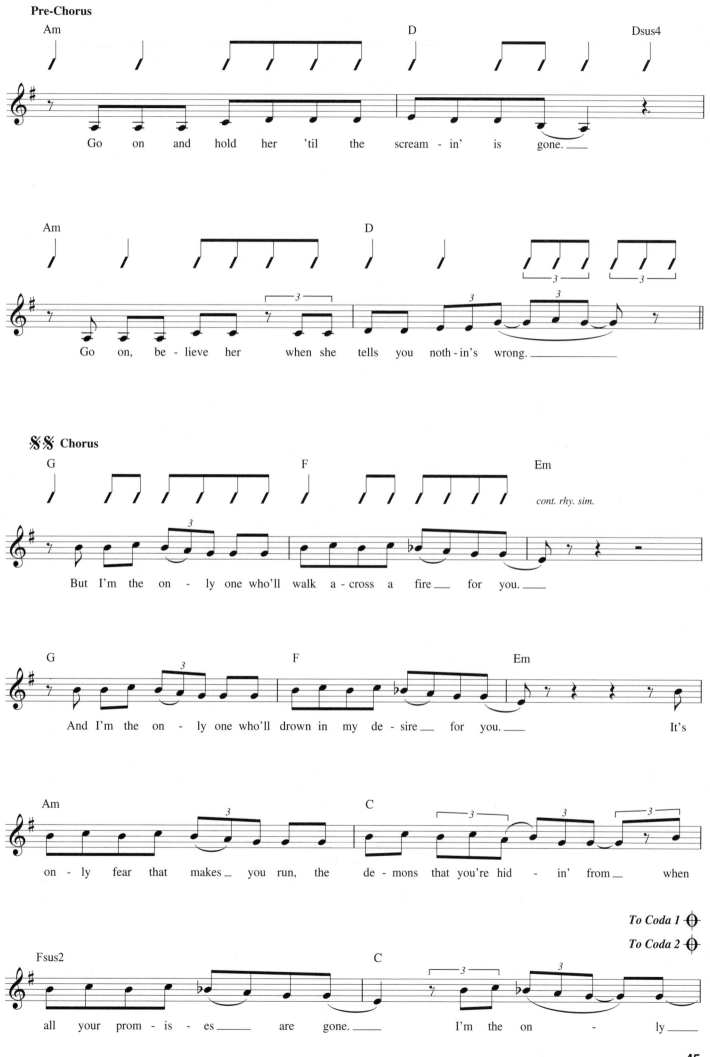

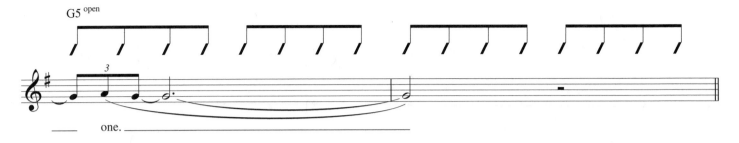

one.

Coda 1

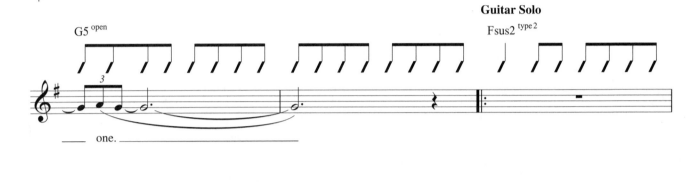

Guitar Solo

one.

cont. rhy. sim.

Pre-Chorus

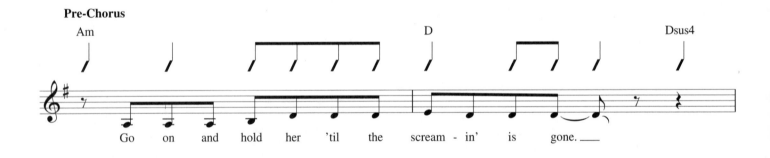

Go on and hold her 'til the scream - in' is gone. ___

Go on be - lieve ___ her when she tells you noth - in's wrong.

Coda 2

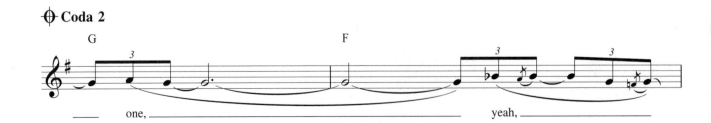

___ one, ___ yeah, ___

Additional Lyrics

2. Please, baby, can't you see I'm tryin' to explain
   I've been here before and I'm lockin' the door
   And I'm not goin' back again.
   Her eyes and arms and skin won't make it go away.
   You'll wake up tomorrow and wrestle the sorrow
   That holds you down today.

Like the Way I Do

Words and Music by Melissa Etheridge

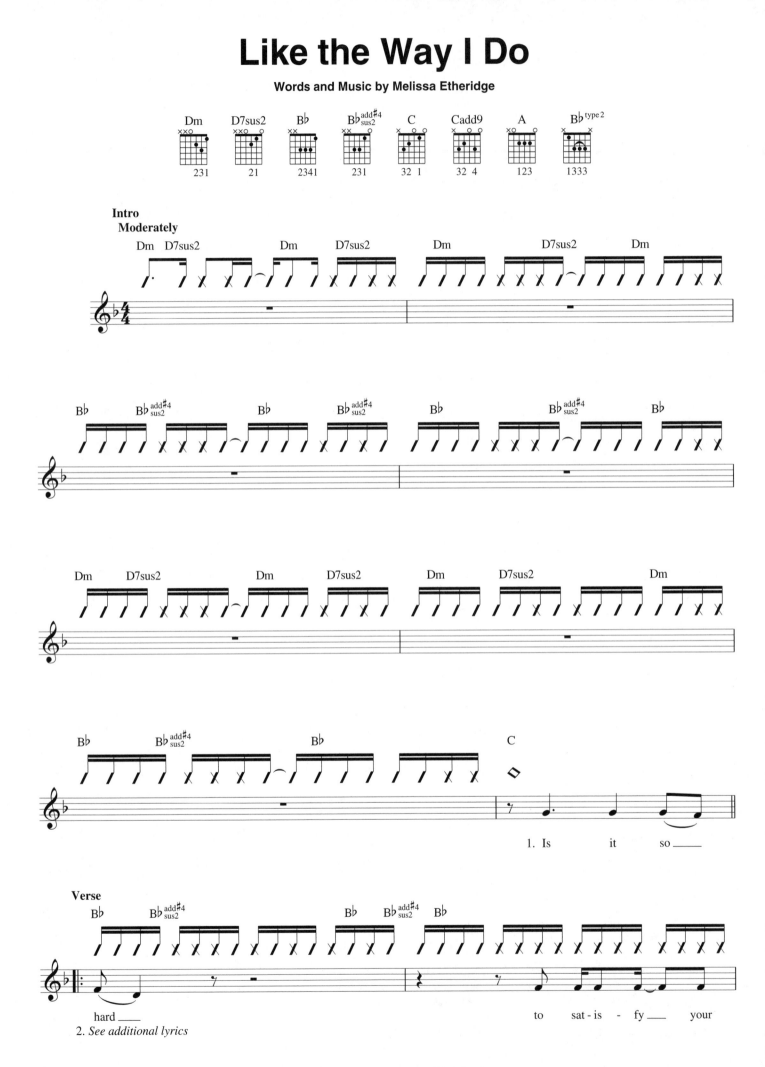

like   I   do.   Ba - by, tell me does she

Chorus

Dm   D7sus2   Dm   D7sus2   Dm   D7sus2   Dm

love   you _   like the way _ I   love   you. _   Does she stim - u - late _

B♭   B♭add#4 sus2   B♭   B♭add#4 sus2   B♭   B♭add#4 sus2   B♭

_ you, _   at-tract and cap - ti-vate you. _   Tell me does she miss _

Cadd9   C   Cadd9   C   Cadd9   C

_ you,   ex - ist - ing just to kiss _ you,   like the way I

Dm D7sus2   Dm   D7sus2   Dm   D7sus2   Dm   D7sus2

do. _   Tell _ me does she

Dm   D7sus2   Dm   D7sus2   Dm   D7sus2   Dm

want   you, _ in - fat - u - ate _ and haunt _ you. _ Does she know just how to _ shock _

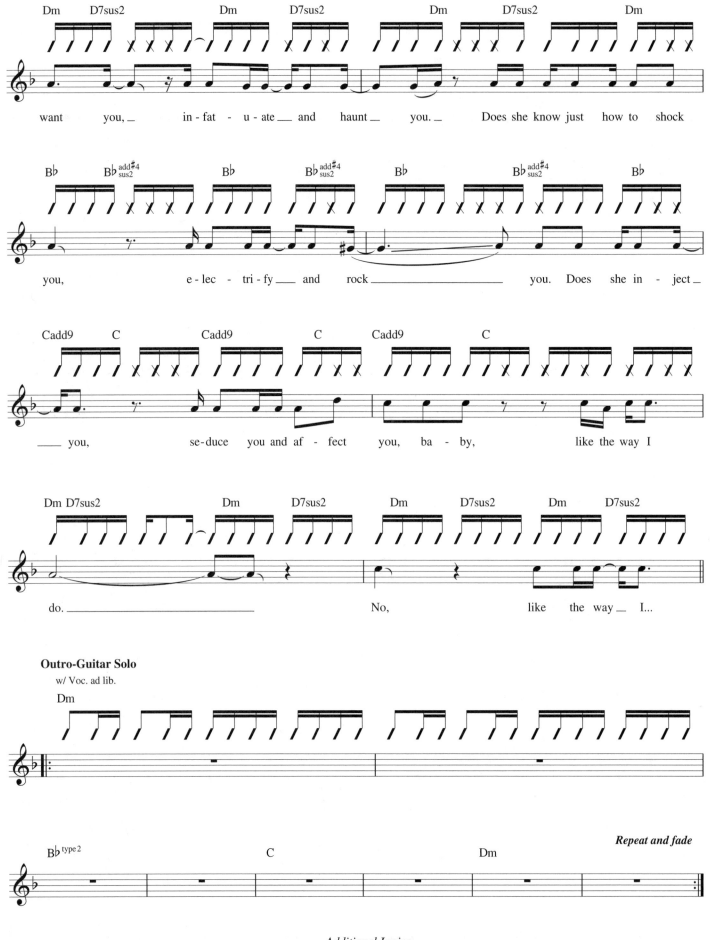

Nowhere to Go

Words and Music by Melissa Etheridge

Additional Lyrics

2. Past the Wal-Mart and the prison, down by the old V.A.,
   Just my jeans and my T-shirt, and my blue Chevrolet.
   Well, it's Saturday night, it feels like ev'rything's wrong.
   I've got some strawberry wine. I want to get you alone, get you alone
   'Cause there's...

3. Down by the muddy water of the mighty Mo,
   In an old abandoned box car. Will I ever know.
   Dance with me forever, this moment is divine.
   I'm so close to heaven, this hell is not mine. This hell is not mine.
   There's...

No Souvenirs

Words and Music by Melissa Etheridge

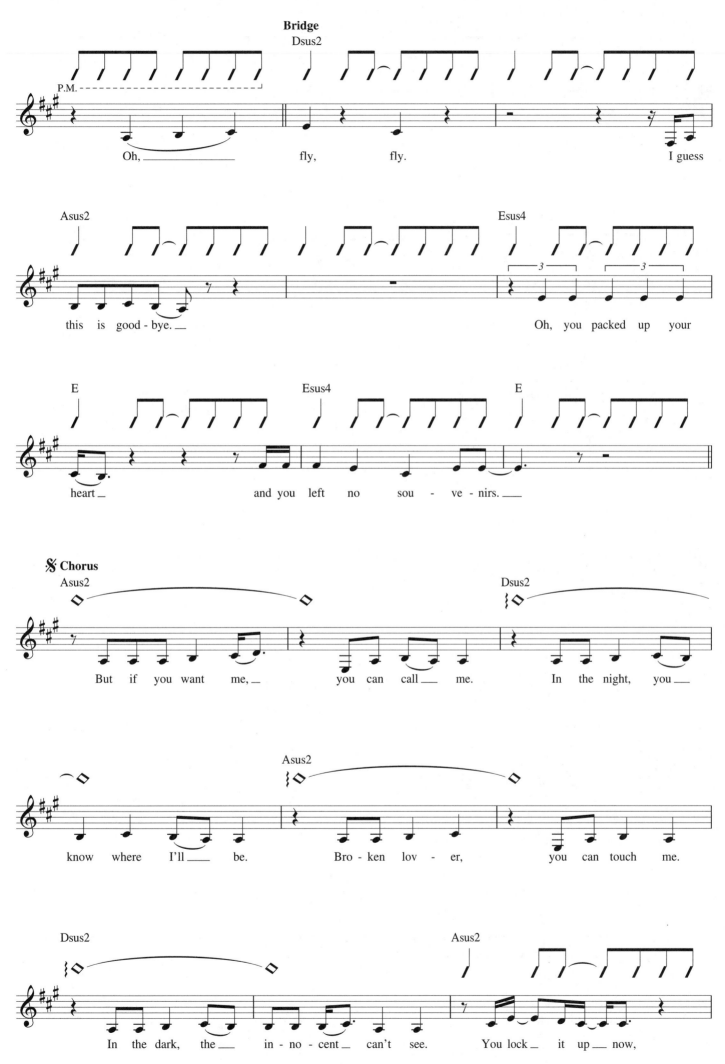

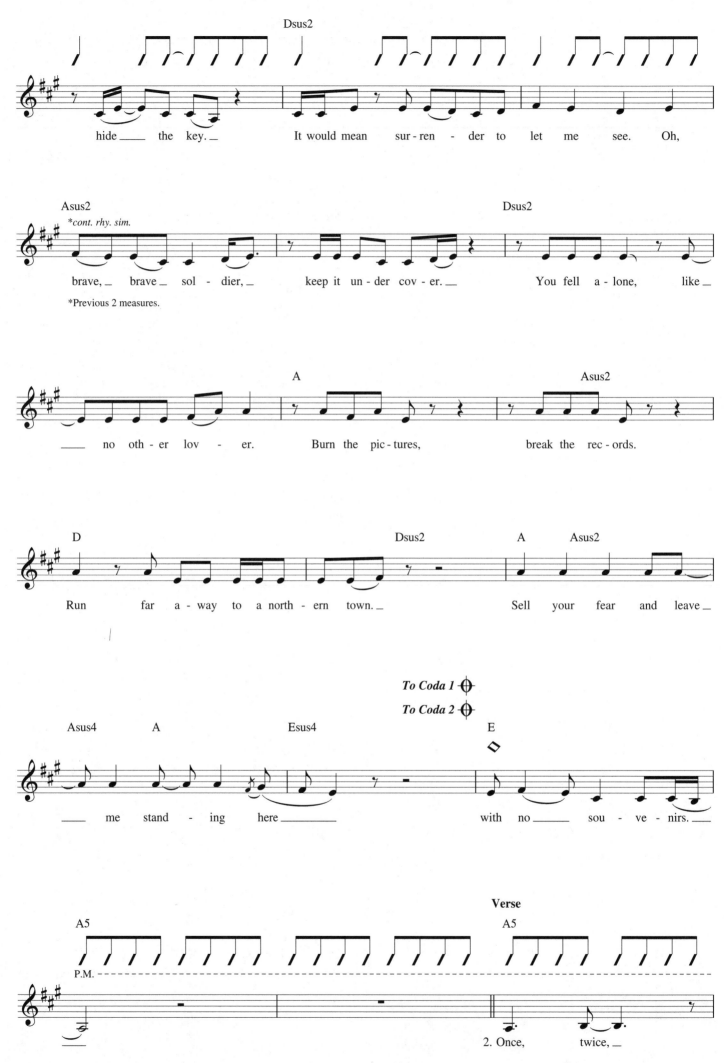

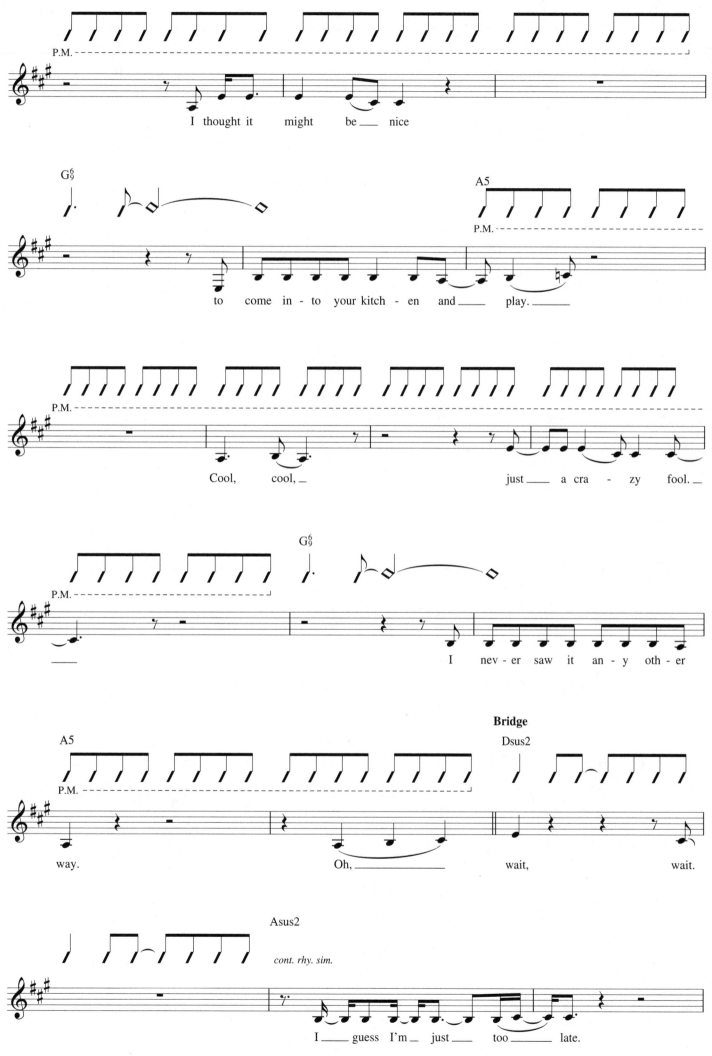

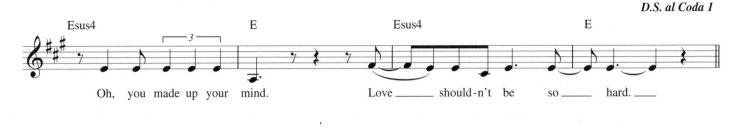

Oh, you made up your mind. Love _____ should-n't be so _____ hard. _____

✛ Coda 1

Interlude

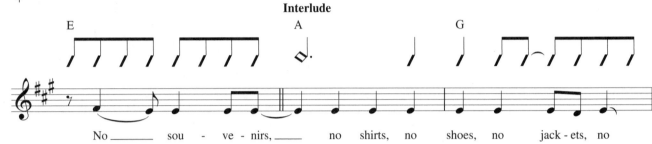

No _____ sou - ve - nirs, _____ no shirts, no shoes, no jack - ets, no

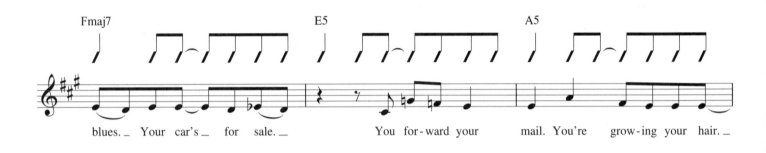

blues. ___ Your car's ___ for sale. ___ You for-ward your mail. You're grow-ing your hair. ___

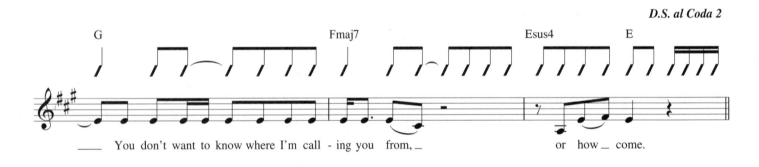

_____ You don't want to know where I'm call - ing you from, ___ or how ___ come.

✛ Coda 2

with no _____ sou - ve - nirs. _____ Yeah. ___

Yeah, _____ hey. _____

D   Dsus2

Asus2

Dsus2

Asus2

Dsus2

A   G$_9^6$ Fmaj7

rit.

Hel - lo,   hel - lo, _____   this is   Ro - me - o. _____

Yes I Am

Words and Music by Melissa Etheridge

1. In these days _____ and these hours _____ of fu - ry, _____

2., 3. *See additional lyrics*

when the dark - ness and an - swers are _____ thin, _____ lov-ers come and check out in a

hur - ry, _____ shal - low _____ and hol-low a - gain.

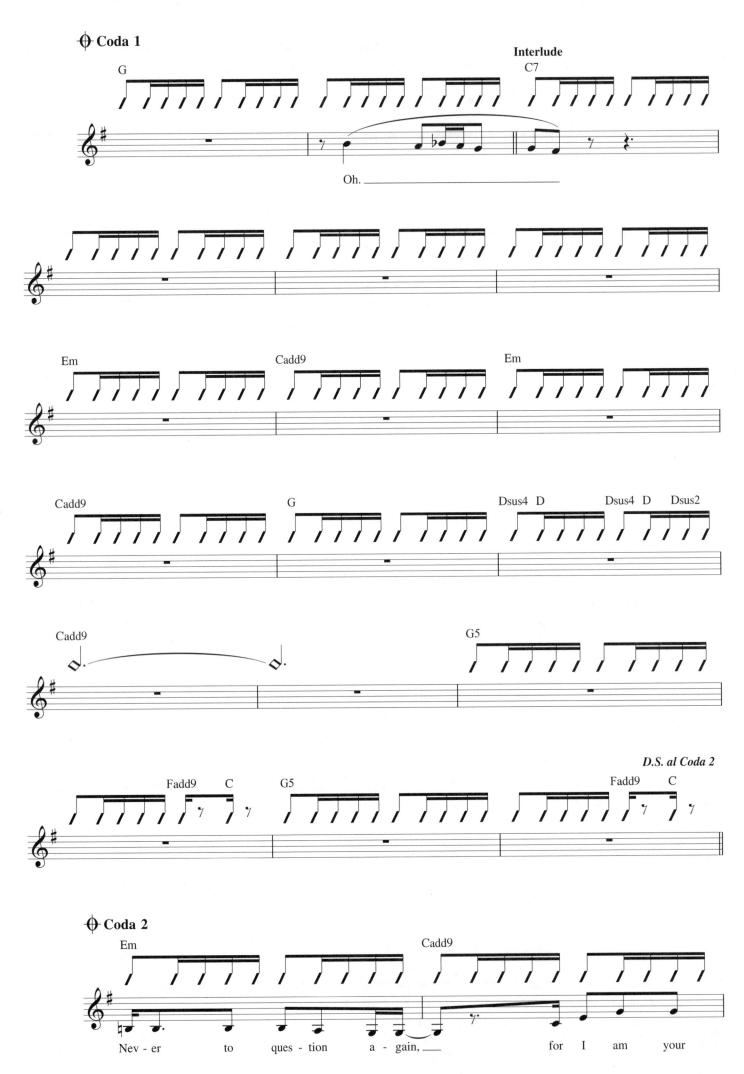

Coda 1

Interlude

G

C7

Oh. _____

Em Cadd9 Em

Cadd9 G Dsus4 D Dsus4 D Dsus2

Cadd9 G5

D.S. al Coda 2

Fadd9 C G5 Fadd9 C

Coda 2

Em Cadd9

Nev - er   to   ques - tion   a - gain, ___   for   I   am   your

Additional Lyrics

2. Barring divine intervention,
   There is nothing between you and I.
   And if I carelessly forgot to mention your body,
   Your power can sanctify.
   Come feed the hunger, the thirst.
   Lay it down, the beast will die.
   You can question my heart once again.
   Am I your passion, your promise, your end.

3. I will stand firm in the tempest.
   I will ride destiny's trail
   To believe when the truth comes up empty,
   To hold and respect without fail.
   Come and be one in the motion.
   A desire they cannot comprehend.
   Never to question again,
   For I am your passion, your promise, your end.

Similar Features

Words and Music by Melissa Etheridge

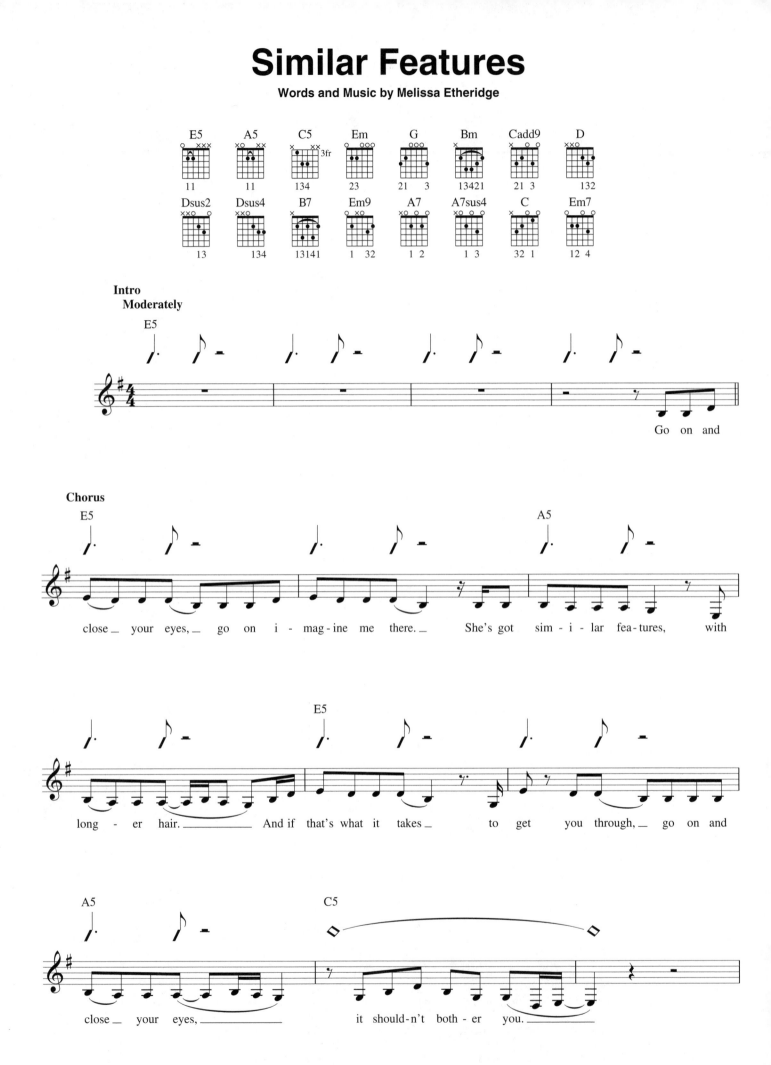

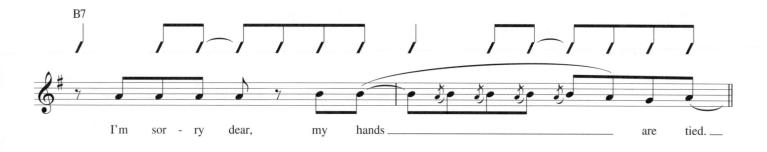

B7

I'm sor - ry dear, my hands _____ are tied. __

Interlude

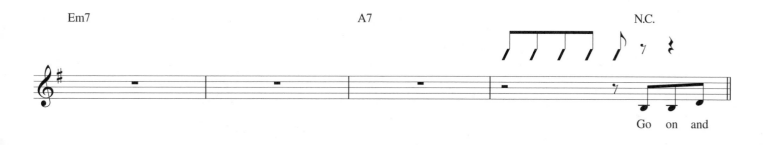

Em7   A7

cont. rhy. sim.

Em7   A7   N.C.

Go on and

Chorus

E5   A5

close __ your eyes, __ go on i - mag-ine me there. __ She's got sim-i-lar fea-tures, with

E5

long - er hair. _____ And if that's what it takes __ to get you through, __ go on and

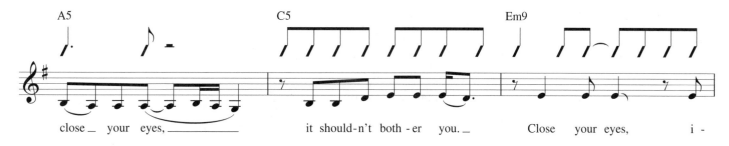

A5   C5   Em9

close __ your eyes, _____ it should-n't both - er you. __ Close your eyes, i -

71

Additional Lyrics

2. Dancing with the wall made you bitter sweet.
   There ain't much you can do when they just lay it at your feet.
   But could you tell by the song I wanted to be the one?
   Did you listen again when the damage was done?
   Now the paint's still wet in your do-it-by number dream.
   Are you gonna tell me how it felt, will you tell me what it means.

Your Little Secret

Words and Music by Melissa Etheridge

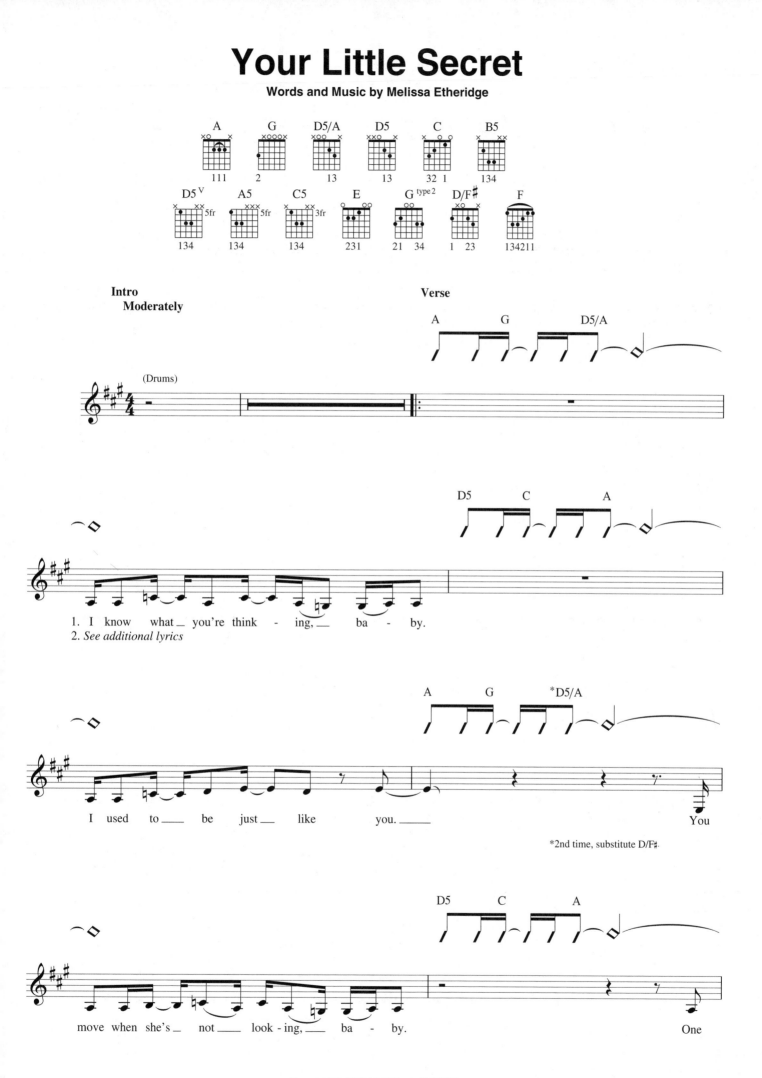

1. I know what you're think - ing, ba - by.
2. *See additional lyrics*

I used to be just like you. You

*2nd time, substitute D/F#.

move when she's not look - ing, ba - by. One

sug-ar ain't e-nough for you, but you, you're tak-ing out your loans.

You're bur-y-ing your bones be-fore your cov-er's blown.

You bet-ter take it home.

Chorus

I like the way you look. I know you like me, but one and one and one, ba-

-by, makes three. Stop play-ing those eyes if

G^type 2   D5/A   1. A

you want me to keep   your lit-tle se - cret, lit-tle se - cret, lit-tle se - cret, yeah.

2. A

cret, lit-tle se - cret, lit-tle se - cret, yeah.

Bridge
E

Lit-tle se - cret, lit-tle se - cret.   I   could,   I   won't,

F   E   F
cont. rhy. sim.
I   can't, __ I   don't. __ You make   it   hard, __ talk   down __ my   guard. __

E   F   E
__ My   sens - es soaked,   my   e - go's choked.   I   will   not   lie, __

F   G^type 2
__ I   will   not   lie.   I,   I,   I,   ho. __

Outro

Lit - tle se - cret, lit - tle se - cret, yeah. Lit - tle se - cret, lit - tle se - cret, yeah.

Lit - tle se - cret, lit - tle se - cret, yeah. Lit - tle se - cret, lit - tle se - cret, now.

Now, now, no, oh! Stop play - ing those eyes.

Whoa!

Additional Lyrics

2. Tell it softly to me, baby,
   That you never meant no one no harm.
   Your wonderland's a mirror, baby.
   It's swiftly fading like your charm,
   But you, you're stepping out of line.
   You're spilling all the wine.
   Leave it on the vine,
   'Cause I can't give you mine.

GUITAR PLAY-ALONG

This series will help you play your favorite songs quickly and easily. Just follow the tab and listen to the CD to hear how the guitar should sound, and then play along using the separate backing tracks. Mac or PC users can also slow down the tempo without changing pitch by using the CD in their computer. The melody and lyrics are included in the book so that you can sing or simply follow along.

1. ROCK
Day Tripper • Message in a Bottle • Refugee • Shattered • Sunshine of Your Love • Takin' Care of Business • Tush • Walk This Way.
00699570 ....$16.99

2. ACOUSTIC
Angie • Behind Blue Eyes • Best of My Love • Blackbird • Dust in the Wind • Layla • Night Moves • Yesterday.
00699569.......................$16.95

3. HARD ROCK
Crazy Train • Iron Man • Living After Midnight • Rock You like a Hurricane • Round and Round • Smoke on the Water • Sweet Child o' Mine • You Really Got Me.
00699573.......................$16.95

4. POP/ROCK
Breakdown • Crazy Little Thing Called Love • Hit Me with Your Best Shot • I Want You to Want Me • Lights • R.O.C.K. in the U.S.A. • Summer of '69 • What I Like About You.
00699571.......................$16.99

5. MODERN ROCK
Aerials • Alive • Bother • Chop Suey! • Control • Last Resort • Take a Look Around (Theme from *M:I-2*) • Wish You Were Here.
00699574 ....$16.99

6. '90s ROCK
Are You Gonna Go My Way • Come out and Play • I'll Stick Around • Know Your Enemy • Man in the Box • Outshined • Smells like Teen Spirit • Under the Bridge.
00699572.......................$16.99

7. BLUES
All Your Love (I Miss Loving) • Born Under a Bad Sign • Hide Away • I'm Tore Down • I'm Your Hoochie Coochie Man • Pride and Joy • Sweet Home Chicago • The Thrill Is Gone.
00699575.......................$16.95

8. ROCK
All Right Now • Black Magic Woman • Get Back • Hey Joe • Layla • Love Me Two Times • Won't Get Fooled Again • You Really Got Me.
00699585.......................$14.95

9. PUNK ROCK
All the Small Things • Fat Lip • Flavor of the Weak • I Feel So • Lifestyles of the Rich and Famous • Say It Ain't So • Self Esteem • (So) Tired of Waiting for You.
00699576.......................$14.95

10. ACOUSTIC
Here Comes the Sun • Landslide • The Magic Bus • Norwegian Wood (This Bird Has Flown) • Pink Houses • Space Oddity • Tangled Up in Blue • Tears in Heaven.
00699586.......................$16.95

11. EARLY ROCK
Fun, Fun, Fun • Hound Dog • Louie, Louie • No Particular Place to Go • Oh, Pretty Woman • Rock Around the Clock • Under the Boardwalk • Wild Thing.
0699579.......................$14.95

12. POP/ROCK
867-5309/Jenny • Every Breath You Take • Money for Nothing • Rebel, Rebel • Run to You • Ticket to Ride • Wonderful Tonight • You Give Love a Bad Name.
00699587.......................$14.95

13. FOLK ROCK
Annie's Song • Leaving on a Jet Plane • Suite: Judy Blue Eyes • This Land Is Your Land • Time in a Bottle • Turn! Turn! Turn! • You've Got a Friend • You've Got to Hide Your Love Away.
00699581.......................$14.95

14. BLUES ROCK
Blue on Black • Crossfire • Cross Road Blues (Crossroads) • The House Is Rockin' • La Grange • Move It on Over • Roadhouse Blues • Statesboro Blues.
00699582.......................$16.95

15. R&B
Ain't Too Proud to Beg • Brick House • Get Ready • I Can't Help Myself • I Got You (I Feel Good) • I Heard It Through the Grapevine • My Girl • Shining Star.
00699583.......................$14.95

16. JAZZ
All Blues • Bluesette • Footprints • How Insensitive • Misty • Satin Doll • Stella by Starlight • Tenor Madness.
00699584.......................$15.95

17. COUNTRY
Amie • Boot Scootin' Boogie • Chattahoochee • Folsom Prison Blues • Friends in Low Places • Forever and Ever, Amen • T-R-O-U-B-L-E • Workin' Man Blues.
00699588.......................$15.95

18. ACOUSTIC ROCK
About a Girl • Breaking the Girl • Drive • Iris • More than Words • Patience • Silent Lucidity • 3 AM.
00699577.......................$15.95

19. SOUL
Get Up (I Feel like Being) a Sex Machine • Green Onions • In the Midnight Hour • Knock on Wood • Mustang Sally • Respect • (Sittin' On) The Dock of the Bay • Soul Man.
00699578.......................$14.95

20. ROCKABILLY
Be-Bop-A-Lula • Blue Suede Shoes • Hello Mary Lou • Little Sister • Mystery Train • Rock This Town • Stray Cat Strut • That'll Be the Day.
00699580.......................$14.95

21. YULETIDE
Angels We Have Heard on High • Away in a Manger • Deck the Hall • The First Noel • Go, Tell It on the Mountain • Jingle Bells • Joy to the World • O Little Town of Bethlehem.
00699602.......................$14.95

22. CHRISTMAS
The Christmas Song • Frosty the Snow Man • Happy Xmas • Here Comes Santa Claus • Jingle-Bell Rock • Merry Christmas, Darling • Rudolph the Red-Nosed Reindeer • Silver Bells.
00699600.......................$15.95

23. SURF
Let's Go Trippin' • Out of Limits • Penetration • Pipeline • Surf City • Surfin' U.S.A. • Walk Don't Run • The Wedge.
00699635.......................$14.95

24. ERIC CLAPTON
Badge • Bell Bottom Blues • Change the World • Cocaine • Key to the Highway • Lay Down Sally • White Room • Wonderful Tonight.
00699649.......................$16.95

25. LENNON & McCARTNEY
Back in the U.S.S.R. • Drive My Car • Get Back • A Hard Day's Night • I Feel Fine • Paperback Writer • Revolution • Ticket to Ride.
00699642 ....$14.95

26. ELVIS PRESLEY
All Shook Up • Blue Suede Shoes • Don't Be Cruel • Heartbreak Hotel • Hound Dog • Jailhouse Rock • Little Sister • Mystery Train.
00699643.......................$14.95

27. DAVID LEE ROTH
Ain't Talkin' 'bout Love • Dance the Night Away • Hot for Teacher • Just like Paradise • A Lil' Ain't Enough • Runnin' with the Devil • Unchained • Yankee Rose.
00699645.......................$16.95

28. GREG KOCH
Chief's Blues • Death of a Bassman • Dylan the Villain • The Grip • Holy Grail • Spank It • Tonus Diabolicus • Zoiks.
00699646.......................$14.95

29. BOB SEGER
Against the Wind • Betty Lou's Gettin' out Tonight • Hollywood Nights • Mainstreet • Night Moves • Old Time Rock & Roll • Rock and Roll Never Forgets • Still the Same.
00699647.......................$14.95

30. KISS
Cold Gin • Detroit Rock City • Deuce • Firehouse • Heaven's on Fire • Love Gun • Rock and Roll All Nite • Shock Me.
00699644.......................$14.95

31. CHRISTMAS HITS
Blue Christmas • Do You Hear What I Hear • Happy Holiday • I Saw Mommy Kissing Santa Claus • I'll Be Home for Christmas • Let It Snow! Let It Snow! Let It Snow! • Little Saint Nick • Snowfall.
00699652.......................$14.95

32. THE OFFSPRING
Bad Habit • Come out and Play • Gone Away • Gotta Get Away • Hit That • The Kids Aren't Alright • Pretty Fly (For a White Guy) • Self Esteem.
00699653.......................$14.95

33. ACOUSTIC CLASSICS
Across the Universe • Babe, I'm Gonna Leave You • Crazy on You • Heart of Gold • Hotel California • I'd Love to Change the World • Thick as a Brick • Wanted Dead or Alive.
00699656.......................$16.95

34. CLASSIC ROCK
Aqualung • Born to Be Wild • The Boys Are Back in Town • Brown Eyed Girl • Reeling in the Years • Rock'n Me • Rocky Mountain Way • Sweet Emotion.
00699658.......................$16.95

35. HAIR METAL
Decadence Dance • Don't Treat Me Bad • Down Boys • Seventeen • Shake Me • Up All Night • Wait • Talk Dirty to Me.
00699660.......................$16.95

36. SOUTHERN ROCK
Can't You See • Flirtin' with Disaster • Hold on Loosely • Jessica • Mississippi Queen • Ramblin' Man • Sweet Home Alabama • What's Your Name.
00699661.......................$16.95

37. ACOUSTIC METAL
Every Rose Has Its Thorn • Fly to the Angels • Hole Hearted • Love Is on the Way • Love of a Lifetime • Signs • To Be with You • When the Children Cry.
00699662.......................$16.95

38. BLUES
Boom Boom • Cold Shot • Crosscut Saw • Everyday I Have the Blues • Frosty • Further on up the Road • Killing Floor • Texas Flood.
00699663.......................$16.95

39. '80s METAL
Bark at the Moon • Big City Nights • Breaking the Chains • Cult of Personality • Lay It Down • Living on a Prayer • Panama • Smokin' in the Boys Room.
00699664.......................$16.99

40. INCUBUS
Are You In? • Drive • Megalomaniac • Nice to Know You • Pardon Me • Stellar • Talk Shows on Mute • Wish You Were Here.
00699668.......................$17.95

41. ERIC CLAPTON
After Midnight • Can't Find My Way Home • Forever Man • I Shot the Sheriff • I'm Tore Down • Pretending • Running on Faith • Tears in Heaven.
00699669.......................$16.95

42. CHART HITS
Are You Gonna Be My Girl • Heaven • Here Without You • I Believe in a Thing Called Love • Just like You • Last Train Home • This Love • Until the Day I Die.
00699670.......................$16.95

43. LYNYRD SKYNYRD
Don't Ask Me No Questions • Free Bird • Gimme Three Steps • I Know a Little • Saturday Night Special • Sweet Home Alabama • That Smell • You Got That Right.
00699681.......................$17.95

44. JAZZ
I Remember You • I'll Remember April • Impressions • In a Mellow Tone • Moonlight in Vermont • On a Slow Boat to China • Things Ain't What They Used to Be • Yesterdays.
00699689........................$14.95

45. TV THEMES
Themes from shows such as: The Addams Family • Hawaii Five-O • King of the Hill • Charlie Brown • Mission: Impossible • The Munsters • The Simpsons • Star Trek®.
00699718........................$14.95

46. MAINSTREAM ROCK
Just a Girl • Keep Away • Kryptonite • Lightning Crashes • 1979 • One Step Closer • Scar Tissue • Torn.
00699722........................$16.95

47. HENDRIX SMASH HITS
All Along the Watchtower • Can You See Me? • Crosstown Traffic • Fire • Foxey Lady • Hey Joe • Manic Depression • Purple Haze • Red House • Remember • Stone Free • The Wind Cries Mary.
00699723........................$19.95

48. AEROSMITH CLASSICS
Back in the Saddle • Draw the Line • Dream On • Last Child • Mama Kin • Same Old Song & Dance • Sweet Emotion • Walk This Way.
00699724........................$16.99

49. STEVIE RAY VAUGHAN
Couldn't Stand the Weather • Empty Arms • Lenny • Little Wing • Look at Little Sister • Love Struck Baby • The Sky Is Crying • Tightrope.
00699725........................$16.95

50. NÜ METAL
Duality • Here to Stay • In the End • Judith • Nookie • So Cold • Toxicity • Whatever.
00699726........................$14.95

51. ALTERNATIVE '90s
Alive • Cherub Rock • Come As You Are • Give It Away • Jane Says • No Excuses • No Rain • Santeria.
00699727........................$12.95

52. FUNK
Cissy Strut • Flashlight • Funk #49 • I Just Want to Celebrate • It's Your Thing • Le Freak • Papa's Got a Brand New Bag • Pick up the Pieces.
00699728........................$14.95

54. HEAVY METAL
Am I Evil? • Back in Black • Holy Diver • Lights Out • The Trooper • You've Got Another Thing Comin' • The Zoo.
00699730........................$14.95

55. POP METAL
Beautiful Girls • Cherry Pie • Get the Funk Out • Here I Go Again • Nothin' but a Good Time • Photograph • Turn up the Radio • We're Not Gonna Take It.
00699731........................$14.95

56. FOO FIGHTERS
All My Life • Best of You • DOA • I'll Stick Around • Learn to Fly • Monkey Wrench • My Hero • This Is a Call.
00699749........................$14.95

57. SYSTEM OF A DOWN
Aerials • B.Y.O.B. • Chop Suey! • Innervision • Question! • Spiders • Sugar • Toxicity.
00699751........................$14.95

58. BLINK-182
Adam's Song • All the Small Things • Dammit • Feeling This • Man Overboard • The Rock Show • Stay Together for the Kids • What's My Age Again?
00699772........................$14.95

59. GODSMACK
Awake • Bad Religion • Greed • I Stand Alone • Keep Away • Running Blind • Straight out of Line • Whatever.
00699773........................$14.95

60. 3 DOORS DOWN
Away from the Sun • Duck and Run • Here Without You • Kryptonite • Let Me Go • Live for Today • Loser • When I'm Gone.
00699774........................$14.95

61. SLIPKNOT
Before I Forget • Duality • The Heretic Anthem • Left Behind • My Plague • Spit It Out • Vermilion • Wait and Bleed.
00699775........................$14.95

62. CHRISTMAS CAROLS
God Rest Ye Merry, Gentlemen • Hark! The Herald Angels Sing • It Came upon the Midnight Clear • O Come, All Ye Faithful (Adeste Fideles) • O Holy Night • Silent Night • We Three Kings of Orient Are • What Child Is This?
00699798........................$12.95

63. CREEDENCE CLEARWATER REVIVAL
Bad Moon Rising • Born on the Bayou • Down on the Corner • Fortunate Son • Green River • Lodi • Proud Mary • Up Around the Bend.
00699802........................$16.99

64. OZZY OSBOURNE
Bark at the Moon • Crazy Train • Flying High Again • Miracle Man • Mr. Crowley • No More Tears • Rock 'N Roll Rebel • Shot in the Dark.
00699803........................$16.99

65. THE DOORS
Break on Through to the Other Side • Hello, I Love You (Won't You Tell Me Your Name?) • L.A. Woman • Light My Fire • Love Me Two Times • People Are Strange • Riders on the Storm • Roadhouse Blues.
00699806........................$16.99

66. THE ROLLING STONES
Beast of Burden • Happy • It's Only Rock 'N Roll (But I Like It) • Miss You • Shattered • She's So Cold • Start Me Up • Tumbling Dice.
00699807........................$16.95

67. BLACK SABBATH
Black Sabbath • Children of the Grave • Iron Man • N.I.B. • Paranoid • Sabbath, Bloody Sabbath • Sweet Leaf • War Pigs (Interpolating Luke's Wall).
00699808........................$16.99

68. PINK FLOYD – DARK SIDE OF THE MOON
Any Colour You Like • Brain Damage • Breathe • Eclipse • Money • Time • Us and Them.
00699809........................$16.99

69. ACOUSTIC FAVORITES
Against the Wind • Band on the Run • Free Fallin' • Have You Ever Seen the Rain? • Love the One You're With • Maggie May • Melissa • Mrs. Robinson.
00699810........................$14.95

71. CHRISTIAN ROCK
All Around Me • Be My Escape • Come on Back to Me • Hands and Feet • Million Pieces • Strong Tower • Tonight • We Are One Tonight.
00699824........................$14.95

72. ACOUSTIC '90s
All Apologies • Daughter • Disarm • Heaven Beside You • My Friends • Name • What I Got • The World I Know.
00699827........................$14.95

74. PAUL BALOCHE
Above All • All the Earth Will Sing Your Praises • Because of Your Love • My Reward • Offering • Open the Eyes of My Heart • Praise Adonai • Rise up and Praise Him.
00699831........................$14.95

75. TOM PETTY
American Girl • I Won't Back Down • Into the Great Wide Open • Learning to Fly • Mary Jane's Last Dance • Refugee • Runnin' Down a Dream • You Don't Know How It Feels.
00699882........................$16.99

76. COUNTRY HITS
Alcohol • Beer for My Horses • Honky Tonk Badonkadonk • It's Five O'Clock Somewhere • Lot of Leavin' Left to Do • Me and My Gang • Pickin' Wildflowers • Summertime.
00699884........................$14.95

78. NIRVANA
All Apologies • Come As You Are • Dumb • Heart Shaped Box • In Bloom • Lithium • Rape Me • Smells like Teen Spirit.
00700132........................$14.95

88. ACOUSTIC ANTHOLOGY
Don't Ask Me Why • Give a Little Bit • Jack and Diane • The Joker • Midnight Rider • Rocky Raccoon • Walk on the Wild Side • and more.
00700175........................$19.95

81. ROCK ANTHOLOGY
Barracuda • Can't Get Enough • Don't Fear the Reaper • Free Ride • Hurts So Good • I Need to Know • Rhiannon • Sultans of Swing • and more.
00700176........................$22.99

82. EASY ROCK SONGS
Bad Case of Loving You • Bang a Gong (Get It On) • I Can't Explain • I Love Rock 'N Roll • La Bamba • Mony, Mony • Should I Stay or Should I Go • Twist and Shout.
00700177........................$12.99

83. THREE CHORD SONGS
Bye Bye Love • Gloria • I Fought the Law • Love Me Do • Mellow Yellow • Stir It Up • Willie and the Hand Jive • You Don't Mess Around with Jim.
00700178........................$12.99

86. BOSTON
Don't Look Back • Long Time • More Than a Feeling • Party • Peace of Mind • Rock & Roll Band • Smokin' • We're Ready.
00700465 ....$16.99

96. THIRD DAY
Blackbird • Call My Name • Consuming Fire • My Hope Is You • Nothing Compares • Tunnel • You Are Mine • Your Love Oh Lord.
00700560........................$14.95

97. ROCK BAND
Are You Gonna Be My Girl • Black Hole Sun • Creep • Dani California • In Bloom • Learn to Fly • Say It Ain't So • When You Were Young.
00700703........................$14.99

98. ROCK BAND
Ballroom Blitz • Detroit Rock City • Don't Fear the Reaper • Highway Star • Mississippi Queen • Should I Stay or Should I Go • Suffragette City • Train Kept A-Rollin'.
00700704........................$14.95

Prices, contents, and availability subject to change without notice.

For complete songlists, visit Hal Leonard online at www.halleonard.com

0509